Anthony Oluwafemi Olaseni **Joshua, OI**
1989, Watford, Hertfordshire, England,
boxer. Anthony is a unified world heavyweight champion,
holding 3 of the 4 major championships : the IBF title since
2016, the WBA (Super) title since 2017, and the WBO title since
March 2018. He has also held the IBO title since 2017, having
previously been the British and Commonwealth heavyweight
champion from 2014 to 2016 at regional level.

Joshua represented England at the World Championships of
2011 as an amateur in the super-heavyweight division, winning
a silver medal, having also represented Great Britain at the
London Olympics the following year, winning gold. A year after
turning professional, he was named Prospect of the Year by The
Ring magazine during 2014.

Anthony's win over long time undisputed World Heavyweight
Champion, Wladimir Klitschko in 2017, was named Fight of the
Year by The Ring magazine and the Boxing Writers Association
of America. Joshua is the 2nd British boxer, after James DeGale,
to win both a gold medal at the Olympics and a world title by a
major professional sanctioning body, also being the first British
heavyweight to achieve the feat. Anthony was ranked as the
world's best active heavyweight by The Ring, the Transnational
Boxing Rankings Board (TBRB), and BoxRec during September
2018. Known for his exceptional punching power, Joshua's won
all but one of his fights to date by knockout.

Anthony is the son of Yeta and Robert Joshua, his mother being
Nigerian, while his father is British with Irish and Nigerian
ancestry, Anthony's Nigerian background having been traced
back to the Yoruba people. His cousin, Ben Lleyemi, is also a

professional boxer, the pair having made their professional debuts together in 2013.

Joshua spent some of his early years in Nigeria as a boarding school student then following his parents' divorce when he was 12, he returned to the UK halfway through Year 7, attending Kings Langley Secondary School. Growing up on the Meriden Estate in Garston, Hertfordshire, he was called "Femi" by his friends and teachers, after his middle name, Oluwafemi. Anthony excelled at football and athletics, having broken his school's Year Nine 100 m record with a time of 11.6 seconds.

A late starter in the sport, Joshua only began boxing during 2007, when aged 18, after his cousin Ben suggested he take it up. His club, Finchley ABC in Barnet, North London, is also home to fellow top professional heavyweight Dereck Chisora. Anthony won the Haringey Box Cup in 2009, which he retained the following year. Joshua won the senior ABA Championships during 2010, in only his 18th bout, again retaining the title 12 months later. He turned down an offer of £50,000 to go professional: "Turning down that £50,000 was easy. I didn't take up the sport for money, I want to win medals."

Anthony's domestic success of 2010 led to a place on the GB Boxing team then later that year he became heavyweight champion at the GB Amateur Boxing Championships after defeating Amin Isa. At the European Amateur Boxing Championships during June 2011, Joshua beat Eric Berechlin and Cathal McMonagle but despite being stopped by aggressive Romanian southpaw Mihai Nistor after receiving several standing counts, he was named Amateur Boxer of the Year that October by the Boxing Writers Club of Great Britain. His amateur record was 40-3.

During the World Amateur Boxing Championships of 2011, in Baku, Azerbaijan, Anthony impressed upon his sudden arrival on the world scene, when he beat Italian reigning World & Olympic champion Roberto Cammarelle then went on to stop Erik Pfeifer of Germany in the semis before losing by a single point to local boxer, Magomedrasul Majidov, winning a silver medal. En route to the final, Joshua secured his place at the Olympic Games in London the following year, in the 91 kg+ division, as a relative newcomer to the elite amateur level of the sport.

Joshua went into the Olympics as a novice on the international scene in 2012, despite being a world silver medalist. He got a tough draw in the last 16 of the super heavyweight competition, being up against Cuban Erislandy Savón, ranked No. 4 in the world by AIBA, nephew of the 3 time Olympic champion Félix Savón. Anthony battled through 3 hard rounds in his opening contest before being given the nod by 17:16.

The decision was controversial, with most observers believing Savon had clearly won the bout, with only a few believing that he'd won on merit. In his next bout he fought 2008 Beijing Olympics silver medalist Zhang Zhilei, dropping his taller opponent in the middle round, helping Joshua to a 15:11 win, guaranteeing at least a bronze medal.

He met Kazakh boxer Ivan Dychko in the semi-finals, where despite Anthony's height disadvantage he won by 13:11 to reach the Olympic final, where he met 32-year-old reigning Olympic Champion and former 2 time World Champion, Roberto Cammarelle of Italy. After losing the first 2 rounds (6:5 and 13:10) to Cammarelle, an opponent he'd already beaten the previous year, Joshua grew into the fight, coming back to level the scores after the third round (18:18), being announced as the winner via count-back to become the new gold medalist, Olympic champion. The outcome was again criticised by some boxing experts, being labeled a "home decision". Anthony was appointed a Member of the Order of the British Empire (MBE) in the 2013 New Year Honours, for services to boxing.

It was confirmed on 11th July 2013 that Joshua had turned professional under the Matchroom Sport promotional banner. Anthony made his professional debut on 5th October that year, at the O2 Arena in London, beating Italian Emanuelue Leo by a first round TKO, the Main-Event of the card featuring Scott Quigg's successful WBA super-bantamweight title defence against Yoandris Salinas.

Joshua's 2nd professional fight was against English heavyweight Paul Butlin, at the Motorpoint Arena in Sheffield, on 26th October 2013. The bout was stopped in the 2nd round when the referee decided Butlin was taking too much punishment, adjudging Joshua the winner by TKO. Anthony's third professional fight was on the Prizefighter Series card against Croatian Hrvoje Kisciek, on 14th November that year, when he got a TKO win in the 2nd round, his third consecutive knockout victory.

Joshua had another 2nd-round TKO victory during February 2014, over Dorian Darch, taking his record to 4-0. The following month Anthony defeated Hector Alfredo Avila with a 1st-round KO, in Glasgow, Scotland, on the undercard of Ricky Burns against Terence Crawford. Joshua then knocked out Matt Legg during the 1st round, on the undercard of Carl Froch vs. George Groves II at Wembley Stadium, during May that year.

In Anthony's 7th professional fight, on 12th July 2014, at the Echo Arena, Liverpool, he defeated Englishman Matt Skelton, via 2nd round stoppage. This was followed in his 8th professional fight, on 13th September 2014, with a 3rd round stoppage victory against German heavyweight Konstantin Airich in the Manchester Arena, taking his record to 8-0.

Joshua was part of the Main-Event of a Matchroom Sport card on 11th October 2014, at The O2 Arena in London, in his 9th professional fight, for the vacant WBC International heavyweight title, against a former champion looking to win the title for a 2nd time, Denis Bakhtov. Anthony won the fight by knockout in the 2nd round, taking his record to 9-0, winning the WBC International heavyweight title, aged just 24.

Joshua defeated Michael Sprott within the 1st round, to extend his record to 10 wins, all by stoppage, on 22nd November 2014. Going into the fight he'd had 9 bouts, none of which had lasted longer than 3 rounds, his total career ring time having been just 35 minutes, 10 seconds, after the bout it was just 36 minutes and 36 seconds, as it lasted only 1 minute 26 seconds.

Anthony was scheduled to face American boxer Kevin Johnson on 31st January 2015 at The O2 Arena in London, but the fight was cancelled after Joshua sustained a back injury. Joshua beat Jason Gavern on 4th April 2015, with a third-round knockout on his return to the ring in Newcastle upon Tyne, Northumberland. In his 12th professional bout on 9th May 2015, Anthony defeated Raphael Zumbano Love, with a 2nd-round knockout in Birmingham, West Midlands.

Joshua defeated former world title challenger Kevin Johnson (29-6-1, 14 KOs), on 30th May 2015, inflicting the first stoppage in Johnson's career. After Kevin was saved by the bell in the first round the fight was stopped by the referee, shortly after the beginning of the second round. Prior to the fight, Johnson had taken WBC Champion, Vitali Klitschko, Tyson Fury and Dereck Chisora the 12-round distance. Kevin announced his retirement a day after the fight, although he made a comeback during March 2017.

It was announced on 16th July 2015 that Anthony would fight the IBO Intercontinental champion, undefeated Scottish boxer Gary Cornish (21-0, 12 KOs) for the vacant Commonwealth heavyweight title at the O2 Arena on 12th September. Joshua won the vacant title by stopping Cornish after just 90 seconds in the first round, Gary being knocked down twice before the fight was stopped. In the post-fight interviews, Anthony said, "Gary had a solid jab, so I had to make sure I didn't take any of those shots. He was throwing a large jab and I tried to slip it. I managed to land the right hand and it was a perfect connection and he went down."

After Joshua stopped Cornish, promoter Barry Hearn confirmed that Dillian Whyte would put his undefeated record on the line against him. Anthony met Whyte in a grudge match for the vacant British heavyweight title on 12th December 2015, whilst also defending his Commonwealth heavyweight title for the first time, the fight taking place on Sky Box Office.

The two had previously fought when still amateurs during 2009, Whyte having won. After surviving the first scare of his professional career during the 2nd round, Joshua won the fight after first shaking Whyte with a right hook to the temple then finishing off with a devastating uppercut for the knockout in the 7th round. Anthony's purse was £3 million for the fight, having signed a 5-year deal with Matchroom, which gave him a share of the Pay Per View revenue.

It was announced during February 2016 that Joshua would face IBF heavyweight champion Charles Martin (23-0-1, 21 KOs) on 9th April 2016, at the O2 Arena. Martin was making the first defence of the belt that he'd won that January, after defeating Vyacheslav Glazkov for the vacant title. Anthony set the pace in the first round, keeping the southpaw at bay before sending him to the canvas with a straight right hand during the 2nd round. Charles got to his feet, only to be knocked down for a 2nd time by a similar punch just moments later. This time Martin failed to beat the 10 count, after taking too long to get to his feet, the referee waving the fight off, with Joshua winning his first world title.

Charles was heavily criticized for his performance, and apparent lack of ambition to win the fight, observers accusing him of quitting early, believing that he could've got up quicker and fought on. Martin later placed the blame on the pre-fight distractions, stating that he was 'mentally not there'. At just 85 days, Martin's reign as IBF heavyweight champion was the 2nd shortest in professional boxing history, with only Tony Tucker's reign during 1987 being shorter.

Promoter Eddie Hearn announced a 3-man shortlist from the IBF's top ranking 15 boxers for Joshua's first defence of his title. This included former WBC heavyweight champion Bermane Stiverne (25-1-2, 21 KOs) and Eric Molina (25-3, 19 KOs), both of whom had been recently beaten by American WBC champion Deontay Wilder, alongside unbeaten upcoming fighter Dominic Breazeale (17-0, 15 KOs).

It was announced on 25th April, that Anthony's next fight would be against the latter on 25th June 2016, at the O2 Arena in London. Breazeale was ranked 13th by the IBF, below the British pair Derek Chisora and David Haye. The week following the announcement of the fight against Dominic, Joshua announced a new multi-fight deal with U.S. broadcaster Showtime, the fight being screened live in the States by Showtime, after they signed up as Anthony's exclusive U.S. partner. The fight averaged 289,000 viewers on Showtime in the afternoon, the card having averaged 227,000.

Breazeale became only the second boxer, after Dillian Whyte, to take Joshua past 3 rounds but after a dominant performance, he successfully defended his IBF heavyweight title with a 7th-round knockout win, Dominic being dropped heavily by a big left hand. After the fight, Eddie Hearn said Anthony could next fight IBF mandatory contender, Joseph Parker, around November.

It was announced during August that Joshua would be making a 2nd defence of his IBF title at the Manchester Arena in Manchester on 26th November, the first time since September 2014 that he'd be fighting in the city. Possible names put forward for the fight were top IBF contenders Kubrat Pulev and Joseph Parker but then former unified heavyweight champion Wladimir Klitschko became the front-runner, after his scheduled rematch with Tyson Fury was cancelled for a 2nd time.

However, a deal couldn't be finalized for Joshua vs. Klitschko, due to the WBA delaying a decision to sanction the fight then Wladimir injuring himself, which put the fight off, although Klitschko said he'd be looking to fight Anthony during the first quarter of 2017. Bryant Jennings and David Price were the names being pushed forward to fight Joshua next, televised in the US live on Showtime. However, it was then announced that Anthony would be fighting at the Manchester Arena, against former world title challenger Eric Molina (25-3, 19 KOs), who was coming off a stoppage victory against Tomasz Adamek, after being behind on the scorecards.

Following 2 one sided rounds, in which Molina hardly threw anything, Joshua knocked Eric out in the third round, after first dropping him with a right hand to the jaw. Molina beat the count but was met with a flurry of punches, forcing referee Steve Gray to step in to end the fight. Nielsen Media Research stated that the fight peaked at 390,000 viewers on Showtime, with an average of 368,000. UK Anti-Doping issued Eric with a two-year ban on 22nd May 2018, backdated from 28th October 2017 - 28th October 2019, after he tested positive for dexamethasone, a corticosteroid, following his loss to Anthony. There was some controversy as Molina had fought twice more during 2017.

The WBA agreed to sanction a unification bout between Joshua and Klitschko for the vacant WBA 'super' title, previously held by Tyson Fury, on 2nd November 2016. The WBA agreement was that if Anthony retained his belt against Eric Molina then the fight would take place on 29th April 2017, at Wembley Stadium in London.

After Joshua knocked out Molina, the Joshua vs. Klitschko fight was officially announced by Hearn in the ring. WBA president Gilberto J. Mendoza confirmed that the winner would have to face mandatory challenger Luis Ortiz next, with deadlines due to be set after the unification fight. However, the following day the IBF announced that the winner must fight their mandatory challenger Kubrat Pulev, so it was believed that either Anthony or Wladimir would have to vacate a title.

Eddie Hearn announced during January 2017 that over 80,000 tickets had been sold, a new box office record, overtaking Carl Froch vs. George Groves II, having put in a request for 5,000 more tickets to be made available. It was reported that Joshua would earn in the region of £15 million for the fight. At the weigh-in, Klitschko weighed in at 240 1/4 lbs, the lightest he'd weighed since 2009, Anthony coming in heavier at 250 lbs.

In front of a post-war record crowd of 90,000, Joshua won by TKO, after a high-drama war that saw both men giving their all. They fought a close and cautious first 4 rounds then in the 5th, Anthony came out roaring, sending Wladimir to the canvas but he angrily got up to dominate Joshua for the remainder of the round, battering him then scoring his own knockdown in round 6.

Over the next few rounds they were again cautious, both men wary of each other, until a reinvigorated Anthony attacked Klitschko in round 11, again sending him to the canvas. Wladimir again rose but Joshua knocked him down for a 2nd time in the round, before unleashing a barrage of punches while Klitschko was against the ropes that made the referee step in to stop the fight.

At the time of stoppage, Anthony was ahead on two judges scorecards 96–93 and 95–93, but the third judge had Wladimir ahead 95–93. CompuBox stats showed that Joshua landed 107 of his 355 punches thrown (30%), while Klitschko landed 94 of 256 (37%). Anthony called out Fury in his post fight interview, "Tyson Fury, where you at, baby? Come on -- that's what they want to see. I just want to fight everyone. I'm really enjoying this right now."

In the press conference after the fight, Joshua said he'd have no issues with having another fight with Klitschko, "I don't mind fighting him again, if he wants the rematch. Big respect to Wladimir for challenging the young lions of the division. It's up to him, I don't mind. As long as Rob thinks it's good I'm good to go." Eddie Hearn said Anthony's next fight would probably take place at the end of the year, possibly at the Principality Stadium in Cardiff.

The fight averaged 659,000 viewers on Showtime in the US, having been shown live, with the fight having begun at c. 5 pm on the east coast and 2 pm Pacific Time. Nielsen Media Research revealed that the fight peaked at 687,000, during rounds 5 - 6, an increase over Joshua's previous Showtime numbers when his fights had been broadcast live during the late afternoon.

The delayed tape-replay on HBO was watched by an average 738,000 viewers, having peaked at 890,000. German TV channel RTL announced that the fight was watched by an average 10.43 million viewers, with the whole card having averaged 9.59 million, which was higher than the 8.91 million that had tuned in to watch Klitschko vs. Fury during 2015.

The IBF granted Anthony an exemption from his mandatory defence on 7th June 2017, allowing a Klitschko rematch, instead of fighting Kubrat Pulev but it wasn't confirmed that the rematch would take place, as Wladimir said he needed time to review his situation before agreeing to another fight. It was only weeks after the bout that Eddie Hearn had filed the paperwork to the IBF to request the exemption to the mandatory defence.

The IBF explained that the rematch must take place no later than 2nd December 2017, with the winner having to fight Pulev next, with no more exemptions. Joshua revealed on 2nd August that he'd need to start a 3-month training camp on 22nd August, if he was to fight on 11th November, hoping a fight with Klitschko would be finalised by then. However, on 3rd August 2017, soon after the IBF granted an exemption, Wladimir announced on his website and social media channels that he was retiring from boxing, thus ending the possibility of a Joshua v Klitschko rematch.

Upon learning that Klitschko had retired, on 4th August the IBF ordered Anthony and 36-year-old Kubrat Pulev (25–1, 13 KOs) to fight next, with a deal having to be reached by 3rd September 2017. The WBA then ordered Joshua to make his mandatory defence against their top ranked fighter Luis Ortiz, giving them 30 days to reach a deal. Barry Hearn stated that the plan was to fight Pulev next, followed by Ortiz, before a potential unification fight against WBC Heavyweight Champion Deontay Wilder. Details being discussed between the camps of Anthony and Kubrat were close to being finalised by 22 August, for the date of 28th October 2017, with Las Vegas as the potential venue.

It was announced on 28 August that Joshua and Pulev would fight at the Principality Stadium in Cardiff, promoter Eddie Hearn stating on 5th September, "I'm delighted that we will be in Cardiff at the magnificent Principality Stadium for the next step of the AJ journey. Nearly 80,000 will gather on Oct. 28th to create another unforgettable night of boxing. Anthony will meet his mandatory challenger, IBF No. 1-ranked Kubrat Pulev, and the card will be stacked with world championship action, domestic title fights and the very best young stars in the game. Get ready for the next episode from the biggest star in world boxing."

The official press conference took place on 11th September, 70,000 tickets having been sold by the following day, making it the fastest ever seller, also setting the record largest indoor boxing attendance. The previous record was for the Muhammad Ali vs. Leon Spinks rematch, which attracted 63,000 fans to the New Orleans Superdrome during 1978.

Joshua's three-fight deal with Showtime had expired, giving Eddie Hearn the chance to talk to other providers, Showtime having had the right of first option and a matching right, if any other networks bid higher. When HBO bid $1.6 million for the rights to show the fight, Showtime matched the bid, so the fight would be shown live in the afternoon on Showtime.

Rumours circulated on 16th October that Pulev had suffered an injury, so the fight could be in jeopardy, reports suggesting that the injury was 10 days old, but Kubrat's camp had kept it quiet. The injury was later confirmed, so 36-year-old Carlos Takam (35-3-1, 27 KOs), who was ranked # 3 by the IBF stepped in to replace Pulev on 12 days notice.

Eddie Hearn said in a statement that he'd received a phone call from Kubrat's promoter Kalle Sauerland, advising him of a shoulder injury that he'd sustained during sparring. Hearn revealed that when the Joshua vs. Pulev fight was made, he contacted Takam's camp, knowing they'd be next in line, telling them to begin a training camp, staying on standby. The IBF stated that Anthony fighting Carlos would satisfy his mandatory defence. Despite Hearn having claimed that Joshua would weigh around 235–240 lbs, he officially weighed a career-heaviest 254 lbs, while Takam came in at 235 lbs.

On fight night, in front of nearly 80,000 fans, Anthony retained his world titles with what many believed was a premature stoppage in round 10, after 1 minute, 34 seconds. Many fans ringside booed the referee, who saw Carlos go out on his feet. After a cagey first round, in the 2nd Takam accidentally headbutted Joshua's nose, his eyes watering.

During round 4, Joshua opened up a cut above Carlos's right eye then after the referee checked the eye, Anthony knocked Takam down with a left hook to the head but Carlos beat the count, surviving the rest of the round. Another cut appeared above Takam's left eye in round 7, referee Phil Edwards asking the ringside doctor to take a look at Carlos a few times during the fight.

During rounds 8 and 9, Joshua started to back off, which saw Takam come forward, landing some good shots to Anthony's head. In round 10, Joshua landed a clean right uppercut, followed by a barrage of punches, so referee Edwards stepped in between them, halting the fight. A doctor confirmed that Anthony's nose wasn't broken, only bruised and swollen.

It was revealed at the time of the stoppage that judges Pawel Kardyni and Michael Alexander had Joshua ahead 89–81, whilst judge Ron McNair had the fight a 90–80 shutout for Joshua. In the post-fight interview, Anthony was asked about the stoppage, who said, "It was a good fight until the ref stopped it, I have the utmost respect for Takam. I have no interest in what's going on with the officials. My job is the opponent. I don't have control over the ref's decision."

Carlos believed the fight was stopped too early, stating that he'd appreciate a rematch. Hearn and Joshua discussed potential fights during 2018, which included fights with Joseph Parker and Deontay Wilder, a win against both making Anthony the undisputed champion, also mentioning an all-British clash against Tyson Fury.

CompuBox stats showed that Joshua landed 152 of 454 punches thrown (34%), Takam having been less busy, connecting with only 52 of his 222 thrown (23%). The fight, which was shown live in the US on Showtime, averaged 334,000 viewers, a replay being shown later in the evening, which averaged 309,000.

It was then reported that Higgins, of Joseph Parker's team, was looking at Lucas Browne as a potential match-up if they failed to land a unification fight with Anthony, stating that a date during March 2018 had been discussed with Joshua's team, but Eddie Hearn offered an 80-20 split, in Joshua's favour. Higgins told Fairfax Media that the offer would need to be improved, taking into consideration that the fight would take place in the UK.

Other names discussed for a fight during the summer of 2018, included Bryant Jennings and Alexander Povetkin. A Tweet from Parker on 15th November '17, stated that he was offered less than half of what was paid to Charles Martin when he defended his IBF title against Joshua. The next day, Higgins told Fairfax Media that he and Hearn were still discussing a deal that would benefit all parties.

Joseph said he was willing to drop to 35% of the net profit then Higgins made a final offer to Hearn on 22nd November, telling

Sky Sports, "It's our final bottom line decision. We feel anything less is disrespectful or a disgrace." Barry stated on 29th November that the fight could be confirmed within a fortnight then Higgins gave Barcelona's Camp Nou as the potential venue.

Hearn said on 11th December that a deal was very close to being announced, with the Principality Stadium, Cardiff a frontrunner to host the fight, Barry jokingly saying that they were over-paying Parker, with the deal being 65-35. Higgins announced on 28th December that a split had been agreed which would see Parker earn between 30-35% of the purse, the fight taking place during April 2018.

Higgins stated that a rematch clause would be in place for Anthony, should he lose, with Parker getting a 55% split. The Principality Stadium in Cardiff was confirmed as the venue for the fight on 8th January 2018, negotiations coming to a close on 14th January, with the fight officially being announced as taking place there on 31st March, live on Sky Sports Box Office.

Showtime announced in an official press release on 5th February that they'd televise the fight live in the US. It was observed on 16th February that Joshua weighed c. 247 lbs, nearly 10 lbs lighter than he'd weighed against Takam. A picture was posted on Twitter which showed the scales that Anthony stood on, his weight being 112.9 kg.

Joshua and Parker both came in lighter compared to their respective previous bouts. Joseph weighed in first at 236.7 lbs, his lightest since he fought Solomon Haumono during July 2016, while Anthony weighed 242.2 lbs, his lightest since 2014, when he fought Michael Sprott. It was reported that Joshua's purse would be a career-high £18 million, with Parker also getting a career-high £8 million.

Anthony was taken the distance for the first time in his 19-0 knockout career, defeating Joseph, via a 12-round unanimous decision to claim the WBO title, while retaining his WBA, IBF and IBO belts. The judges scored the fight 118–110, 118–110, and 119–109 in favour of Joshua, while many media outlets, including ESPN, had the fight c. 116–112, with Anthony the clear winner.

By going the distance, Joshua's 20 fight knockout streak came to an end. Parker used his movement well to slip a lot of Anthony's attacks but didn't do enough himself to win more rounds. Joseph started on the backfoot in the opening rounds, allowing Joshua to take them. There was an accidental clash of heads in round 3, but neither boxer was cut.

There was another accidental head-butt in round 9, when the referee called for a short break. Anthony's tape on his left glove kept coming loose, so he was instructed to go back to his corner for a re-tape. Parker suffered a cut over his left eye after Joshua accidentally elbowed him. In the final round neither boxer engaged as much as expected, with Anthony trying to close Joseph down, who again on the backfoot, tried to survive the round.

The fight was marred by Italian referee Giuseppe Quartarone, who kept both boxers from fighting on the inside, which mainly had negative impact on Parker, as that was where he had most of his success. The referee broke the action each time both boxers were on the inside, even when they were still throwing shots. Many boxers, pundits and both the Sky Sports and Showtime broadcast team criticised the referee during and after the fight.

After the fight, Joshua discussed his game plan, "My strategy in there was kind of stick behind the jab. It's one of the most important weapons. The old saying is the right hand could take you around the block, but a good jab will take you around the world, and that secured another championship belt. So I stuck behind the jab and I made sure anything that was coming back, I was switched on, I was focused and 12 rounds, baby! I thought it was hard, right?"

Joseph was humble in defeat, stating that he would back stronger, "Today I got beaten by a better champion, bigger man. A lot to work on. It was a good experience being here. Thank you all for the opportunity to fight in this big stadium. We're gonna go back, train hard, plan again and come back stronger. No regrets, you know, take it on the chin. ... So we'll be back again."

When asked what he would do different, Parker replied, "Work harder. Come back stronger, more punches, but I would love to have another go. Just back to the drawing board." During the post fight press conference, Joseph's team stated that the referee didn't speak English, whereas Anthony and his promoter Barry Hearn disagreed, saying that he spoke English fluently. Compubox Punch stats showed that Joshua landed 139 of 383 punches thrown (36.3%), while Parker landed 101 of his 492 thrown (20.5%).

The fight was shown live in the US on Showtime in the afternoon, averaging 346,000 viewers, having peaked at 379,000. A replay was shown later in the evening when the replay averaged 430,000 viewers, peaking at 483,000. Nielsen Media Research, who released the figures didn't have the facilities to measure whether the same customers that watched the live showing tuned in for the replay.

Both the Joshua and Deontay Wilder camps were involved in intensive talks from April - the end of June 2018, aimed at fixing the super fight to finally take place, the main hurdles being split, date and venue. At one point Wilder had agreed to fight Anthony in the UK, but there was some confusion in the contracts that were being sent back and forth.

At the same time, Hearn was also working a deal out for Joshua to fight WBA mandatory challenger Alexander Povetkin (34-1, 24 KOs), the WBA having first ordered the fight after Povetkin knocked out David Price on the Joshua-Parker undercard. Negotiations speeded up on 26th June, when the WBA gave Anthony's camp 24 hours to finalise a deal with Alexander. With Joshua closer to fighting Povetkin in September 2018, Hearn stated that the Joshua-Wilder fight would take place during April 2019 at Wembley Stadium. Barry later stated that the WBA would've granted an exemption, had Deontay signed a deal to fight Anthony.

On Hearn announced on 5th July '18 that Wembley Stadium in London would host Joshua's next two fights, on 22nd September 2018 then 13th April 2019. Joshua vs. Povetkin for the WBA, IBF, WBO and IBO heavyweight titles was officially announced on 16th July as taking place on 22nd September, screened by Sky Box Office. Many British pundits and trainers stated that Anthony shouldn't underestimate Alexander, who was expected to pose a big threat to Joshua.

Anthony signed a new 3-year deal with Matchroom Boxing on 27th July, for him to be on Sky Box Office for at least another 5 fights, including the bout with Povetkin. It was revealed on 1st

August by the WBO that the bout against Alexander would satisfy Joshua's mandatory defences for both the WBA and WBO, as Povetkin was ranked at # 1 by both governing bodies. It was also announced that Anthony would be named the Super Champion should he defeat Alexander.

With nearly 80,000 in attendance, Joshua knocked out Povetkin in round 7 to retain his world titles, on 22nd September. Using his good movement, weaving in and out, Alexander had Anthony hurt early on with his big shots. In round 2, Joshua's nose began to bruise but from round 5 Povetkin began to tire then Anthony dropped him with a left hand to the head in round 7. Alexander got back up but Joshua went straight back in with a flurry of hard shots, before the referee stopped the fight. At the time of stoppage, the 3 judges scorecards were 58–56, 58–56, and 59–55 in favour of Anthony, although the scores didn't seem to reflect Povetkin's success earlier in the fight.

In his post-fight interview, Joshua stated, "I've got my knockout streak back and I found my right hand again. Alexander Povetkin is a very tough challenge. He provided that, he was good with the left hook. I realized he was strong to the head but weak to the body, so I was switching it up. Every jab takes a breath out of you and I slowed him down."

Anthony then stated that he'd post a poll on Twitter asking the fans who they'd like to see him fight next. Compubox Punch stats showed that Joshua landed 90 of 256 punches thrown (35%), with 53 of them landed being jabs. Alexander landed 47 of his 181 thrown (26%) but connected with 43 power shots compared to Joshua's 37. There was a big size advantage in favour of Anthony, who weighed 246 lbs to Povetkin's 222 lbs.

Joshua was reported as making c. £20 million and Alexander c. £6 million from the fight.

Anthony has expressed an interest in chess and reading, as ways to reinforce his boxing and tactical abilities. He was a bricklayer before taking up boxing full-time. Joshua was put on remand in Reading Prison during 2009, for what he describes as "fighting and other crazy stuff", having had to wear an electronic tag on his ankle when released.

Anthony was pulled over by the police for speeding in Colindale, North London, during March 2011, being found with 8 ounces of herbal cannabis hidden in a sports bag in his Mercedes-Benz. He was charged with possession, with intent to supply a class B drug, an offence that carried a maximum 14-year sentence. Joshua was suspended from the GB boxing squad, being sentenced to a 12-month community order and 100 hours' unpaid work, after pleading guilty at crown court.

Anthony announced during November 2016 that he'd be investing in a members-only fitness gym, BXR. Joshua teamed up with the founders of BXR via his physio and medical contacts, the same team from CHHP London in Harley Street being available at BXR, including a number of sports therapists, physiotherapists, doctors and osteopaths alongside BXR's boxers, boxing coaches and Mixed Martial Arts fighters. The gym opened during January 2017 on Chiltern Street, in Marylebone, London.

Professional boxing record

Professional record summary

22 fights		22 wins 0 losses			
By knockout	21	0			
By decision	1	0			

No.	Result	Record	Opponent	Type	Round, time
	Date	Location		Notes	

22	Win	22–0	Alexander Povetkin	TKO	7 (12),

1:59 22 Sep 2018 Wembley Stadium, London, England
Retained WBA (Super), IBF, WBO, and IBO heavyweight titles

21	Win	21–0	Joseph Parker UD	12	31 Mar

2018 Principality Stadium, Cardiff, Wales Retained WBA (Super), IBF, and IBO heavyweight titles;

Won WBO heavyweight title

20	Win	20–0	Carlos Takam TKO	10 (12), 1:34

28 Oct 2017 Principality Stadium, Cardiff, Wales
Retained WBA (Super), IBF, and IBO heavyweight titles

19	Win	19–0	Wladimir Klitschko	TKO	11 (12),

2:25 29 Apr 2017 Wembley Stadium, London, England
Retained IBF heavyweight title;

Won vacant WBA (Super) and IBO heavyweight titles

18	Win	18–0	Éric Molina TKO	3 (12), 2:02

10 Dec 2016 Manchester Arena, Manchester, EnglandRetained IBF heavyweight title

17   Win   17–0   Dominic Breazeale   TKO   7 (12), 1:01   25 Jun 2016   The O2 Arena, London, England
Retained IBF heavyweight title

16   Win   16–0   Charles Martin KO   2 (12), 1:32
9 Apr 2016   The O2 Arena, London, England
Won IBF heavyweight title

15   Win   15–0   Dillian Whyte   KO   7 (12), 1:27
12 Dec 2015   The O2 Arena, London, England
Retained WBC International and Commonwealth
heavyweight titles;

Won vacant British heavyweight title

14   Win   14–0   Gary Cornish   TKO   1 (12), 1:37
12 Sep 2015   The O2 Arena, London, England
Retained WBC International heavyweight title;

Won vacant Commonwealth heavyweight title

13   Win   13–0   Kevin Johnson   TKO   2 (10), 1:22
30 May 2015   The O2 Arena, London, England
Retained WBC International heavyweight title

12   Win   12–0   Raphael Zumbano Love   TKO
2 (8), 1:21   9 May 2015   Barclaycard Arena,
Birmingham, England

11   Win   11–0   Jason Gavern   KO   3 (8), 1:21 4 Apr
2015   Metro Radio Arena, Newcastle, England

10   Win   10–0   Michael Sprott TKO   1 (10), 1:26
22 Nov 2014   Echo Arena, Liverpool, England

9	Win	9–0	Denis Bakhtov TKO	2 (10), 1:00
	11 Oct 2014		The O2 Arena, London, England	
	Won vacant WBC International heavyweight title			

8	Win	8–0	Konstantin Airich	TKO	3 (8),
1:16	13 Sep 2014		Phones 4u Arena, Manchester,	
England				

| 7 | Win | 7–0 | Matt Skelton TKO | 2 (6), 2:33 |
| | 12 Jul 2014 | | Echo Arena, Liverpool, England | |

| 6 | Win | 6–0 | Matt Legg KO | 1 (6), 1:23 |
| | 31 May 2014 | | Wembley Stadium, London, England | |

5	Win	5–0	Hector Avila KO	1 (6), 2:14
	1 Mar 2014		Exhibition and Conference Centre,	
Glasgow, Scotland				

| 4 | Win | 4–0 | Dorian Darch TKO | 2 (6), 0:51 |
| | 1 Feb 2014 | | Motorpoint Arena, Cardiff, Wales | |

| 3 | Win | 3–0 | Hrvoje Kisicek TKO | 2 (6), 1:38 |
| | 14 Nov 2013 | | York Hall, London, England | |

| 2 | Win | 2–0 | Paul Butlin TKO | 2 (6), 0:50 |
| | 26 Oct 2013 | | Motorpoint Arena, Sheffield, England | |

| 1 | Win | 1–0 | Emanuele Leo TKO | 1 (6), 2:47 |
| | 5 Oct 2013 | | The O2 Arena, London, England | |

Pay-per-view bouts

Date	Fight	Network Source(s)	Pay-per-view buys

12 December 2015   Anthony Joshua vs. Dillian Whyte
        Sky Box Office   420,000

9 April 2016   Anthony Joshua vs. Charles Martin   Sky Box
Office   500,000

25 June 2016   Anthony Joshua vs. Dominic Breazeale Sky Box
Office   512,000

10 December 2016   Anthony Joshua vs. Éric Molina Sky Box
Office   450,000

29 April 2017   Anthony Joshua vs. Wladimir Klitschko   Sky Box
Office   1,532,000

28 October 2017   Anthony Joshua vs. Carlos Takam
        Sky Box Office   887,000

31 March 2018 Anthony Joshua vs. Joseph Parker   Sky
Box Office   1,457,000

22 September 2018   Anthony Joshua vs. Alexander Povetkin
        Sky Box Office   1,113,000

Total sales   Sky Box Office   6,871,000

Amateur highlights

2009 as a Super Heavyweight. Results were:

Lost to Dillian Whyte (United Kingdom) UD-3

2010 won the ABA National Championships 91 kg+ in Bethnal Green, London as a Super Heavyweight. Results were:

Defeated Chris Duff (United Kingdom) WO

Defeated Simon Hadden (United Kingdom) WO

Defeated Dominic Winrow (Isle of Man) RSC-1

2010 won the Haringey International Tournament in Haringey, London as a Super Heavyweight. Results were:

Defeated Otto Wallin (Sweden) PTS

2011 won the ABA National Championships 91 kg+ in Colchester, Essex as a Super Heavyweight. Results were:

Defeated Fayz Aboadi Abbas (United Kingdom) PTS (24-15)

2011 came 7th in the 39th European Amateur Boxing Championships 91 kg+ in Ankara, Turkey as a Super Heavyweight. Results were:

Defeated Eric (Germany) PTS (23-16)

Defeated Cathal McMonagle (Ireland) PTS (22-10)

Lost to Mihai Nistor (Romania) RSCH-3

2011 came 2nd in the 16th 2011 AIBA World Boxing Championships 91 kg+ in Baku, Azerbaijan as a Super Heavyweight. Results were:

Defeated Tariq Abdul-Haqq (Trinidad and Tobago) RSCI-3

Defeated Juan Isidro Hiracheta (Mexico) RET-1

Defeated Mohamed Arjaoui (Morocco) PTS (16-7)

Defeated Roberto Cammarelle (Italy) PTS (15-13)

Defeated Erik Pfeiffer (Germany) RSCI-1

Lost to Magomedrasul Medzhidov (Azerbaijan) PTS (22-21)

2012 Super Heavyweight Olympic Gold Medalist as a member of Team GB. His results were:

Defeated Erislandy Savón (Cuba) PTS (17-16)

Defeated Zhang Zhilei (China) PTS (15:11)

Defeated Ivan Dychko (Kazakhstan) PTS (13-11)

Defeated Roberto Cammarelle (Italy) PTS (+18-18)

Sporting positions

Amateur boxing titles

Previous:

Simon Vallily   ABA super-heavyweight champion

2010, 2011   Next:

Joe Joyce

Previous:

Roberto Cammarelle   Olympic super-heavyweight champion

2012   Next:

Tony Yoka

Regional boxing titles

Vacant

Title last held by

Alexander Povetkin   WBC International

heavyweight champion

30 May 2014 – 9 April 2016

Vacated   Vacant

Title next held by

Dillian Whyte

Vacant

Title last held by

Lucas Browne   Commonwealth heavyweight champion

12 September 2015 – 9 April 2016

Vacated   Vacant

Title next held by

Lenroy Thomas

Vacant

Title last held by

Tyson Fury   British heavyweight champion

12 December 2015 − 9 April 2016

Vacated   Vacant

Title next held by

Dillian Whyte

Minor world boxing titles

Vacant

Title last held by

Tyson Fury   IBO heavyweight champion

29 April 2017 − present Incumbent

Major world boxing titles

Preceded by

Charles Martin IBF heavyweight champion

9 April 2016 − present   Incumbent

Vacant

Title last held by

Tyson Fury

as Unified champion   WBA heavyweight champion

Super title

29 April 2017 − present

Preceded by

Joseph Parker   WBO heavyweight champion

31 March 2018 – present

Awards

Previous:

Vasyl Lomachenko   The Ring Prospect of the Year

2014   Next:

Takuma Inoue

Previous:

Francisco Vargas vs.

Orlando Salido The Ring Fight of the Year

vs. Wladimir Klitschko

2017   Incumbent

BWAA Fight of the Year

vs. Wladimir Klitschko

2017

ESPN Fight of the Year

vs. Wladimir Klitschko

2017

Previous:

Dillian Whyte vs.

Dereck Chisora

Round 5   ESPN Round of the Year

vs. Wladimir Klitschko

Round 5

2017

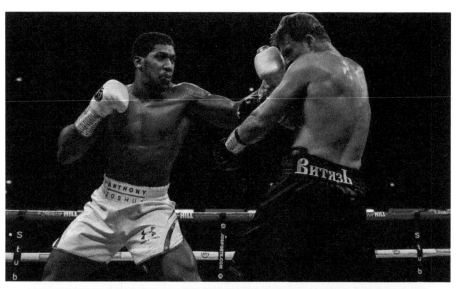

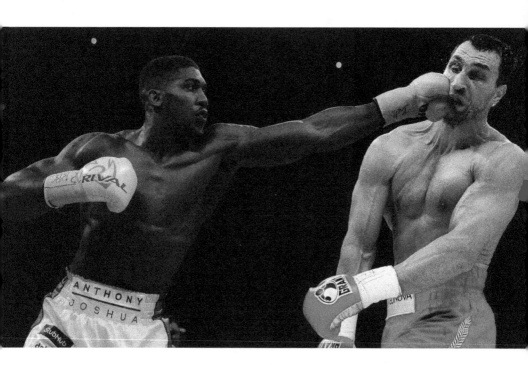

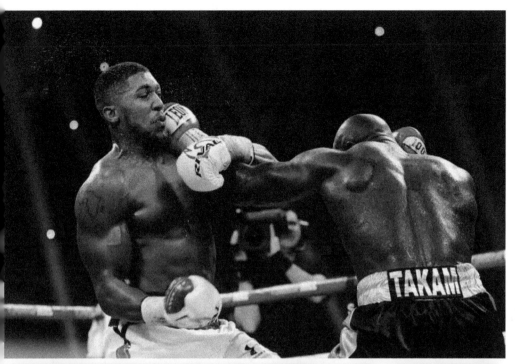

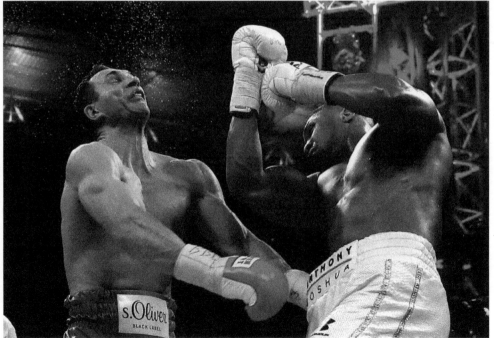

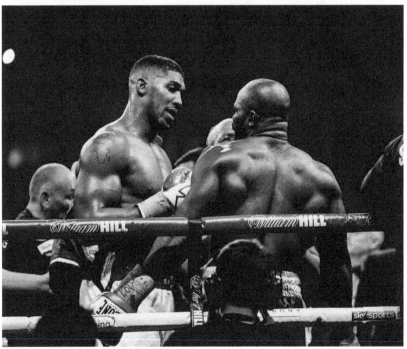

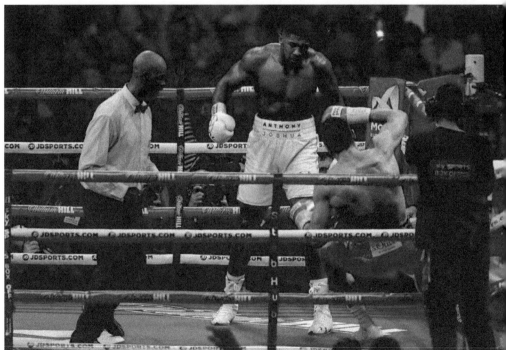

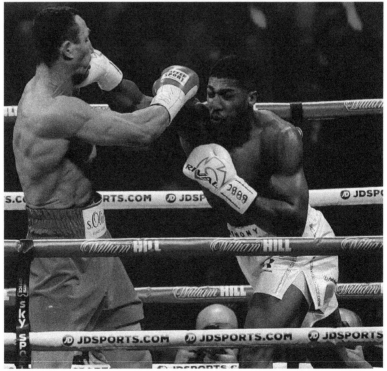

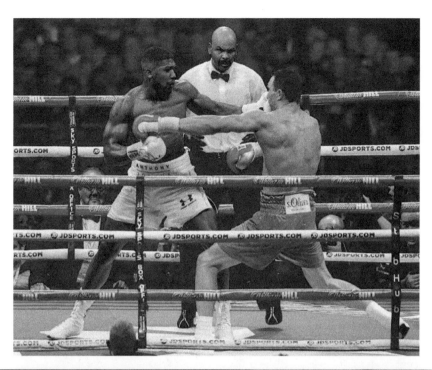

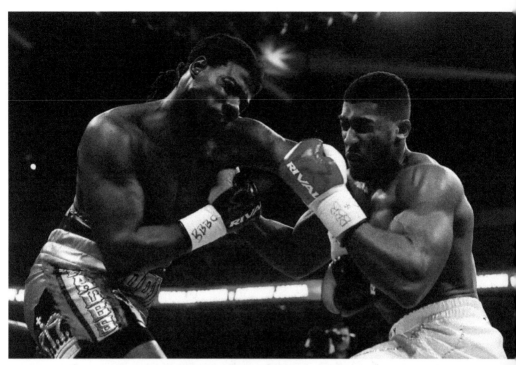

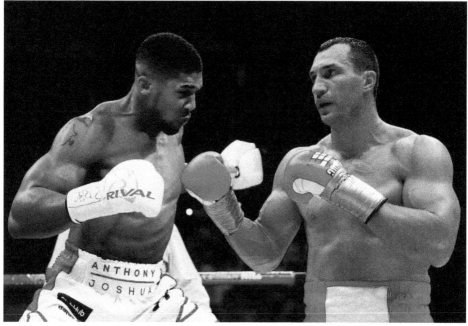

96

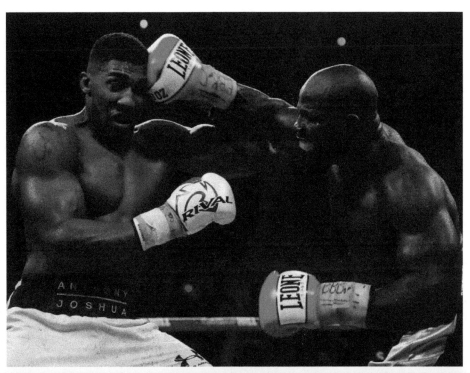